Puppy Love

First Edition
27 26 25 24 23   5 4 3 2 1

Text © 2023 Gibbs Smith
Illustrations © 2023 Sara Mulvanny

Published by
Gibbs Smith
P.O. Box 667
Layton, Utah 84041

1.800.835.4993 orders
www.gibbs-smith.com

Designer: Virginia Snow
Art director: Ryan Thomann
Editor: Gleni Bartels
Production manager: Felix Gregorio
Printed and bound in China by RR Donnelley Asia Printing Solutions

Gibbs Smith books are printed on either recycled, 100% post-
consumer waste, FSC-certified papers or on paper produced from
sustainable PEFC-certified forest/controlled wood source. Learn more
at www.pefc.org.

Library of Congress Control Number: 2022046883

ISBN: 978-1-4236-6354-6

PUPPY LOVE

An Illustrated Guide to
Picking Your Perfect Canine Companion

by Melissa Maxwell
illustrated by Sara Mulvanny

Gibbs Smith

Contents

Pawfect Match Quiz

Quick Rufference Guide

Looking for love can be hard.

Sometimes it feels like all the good ones are taken, and you start to wonder if you'll ever find the One. And then, when you do catch feelings, how do you make it last? What if they don't get along with your family and friends? What if they're jealous and possessive? What if they drink from the toilet bowl, chew up your favorite shoes, and eat their own vomit?

Oh, did you think we were talking about humans? Then you're barking up the wrong tree. This book is all about making a meaningful match with an un-fur-gettable pooch. Being single doesn't have to be ruff. There are a lot of good boys and girls in this great big dog park we call life! Whether you're looking for pointers on Pointers (page 65) or the inside scoop on amount of poop you'll have to scoop, this book has you covered. You'll find where to meet the love of your life, tips for keeping a healthy relationship, and how to avoid furry fails. There are also 42 profiles of some of the most popular breeds to give you a glimpse of what's out there.

When it comes to puppy love, anything is paws-ible!

Are You Ready to Put Yourself Out There?

In the human dating world, "putting yourself out there" means being transparent about who you are, what you're looking for, and how you feel, and that same honesty is needed when it comes to finding furry friends. Before diving into the doggy dating scene and falling for the first cute canine you see, ask yourself if you're doing it for the right reasons. Here are some things to consider if you're seeking a slobbery soulmate:

Set realistic expectations. This is a serious responsibility, so ask yourself some serious questions: Can you commit? Can you afford the lifetime costs of dog ownership? (Spoiler alert: It's not cheap.) Can you clear your calendar to train, exercise, and devote time to your puppy pal?

Know what you want. You don't need to have an exact type, but it's essential to do your research. The good news is you've already started by reading this book! Just like human dating, you may find yourself attracted to certain features—but are they really compatible with your lifestyle? Spend time figuring out which dogs are best suited to your living arrangements (apartment or house), your surrounding environment (city or countryside), your activity level, and your family dynamic (small children or other pets). The quiz on page 104 can help you determine your priorities and give you some breeds that fit the bill.

Accept relationship baggage. Most partners come with a dating history and emotional baggage. Pup partnership is no different. Understand that your dog may have trust issues from unfaithful ex-owners and behavioral problems that stem from fear. Acknowledge and unpack your own baggage, too, when you're considering a canine commitment.

Look out for red flags. How someone acts on a first date may not always indicate how they'll be in a relationship. While you might fall for a pup's playfulness when you meet them in a shelter, that energy can wreak havoc on your peaceful home when you're together 24/7. Notice the signs and be prepared to deal with them.

Take control of your destiny. Proper planning doesn't mean you're not a romantic. If anything, it's the opposite. Understanding yourself and being deliberate in your search improves your chances of finding the right connection. You can create your own happy ending and live puppily ever after.

Where to Meet Cute Singles

Once you know what you're looking for and the doggy deal breakers you're not, it's time to start your search. Nowadays, you have many options for finding Fido, but here are some of the hottest spots to spot a Spot.

SHELTERS & RESCUES

The best way to ensure you're getting your permanent plus-one from a trusted source is to find an animal shelter or animal rescue. Most cities, towns, and counties have a shelter or humane society that takes in stray doggos and pooches who have been relinquished by their erstwhile owners. The folks who devote their time to rescues are dedicated and passionate matchmakers, and they usually have a more rigorous screening process than the other places on this list.

You can always visit local rescues and shelters in person (or even better, volunteer at one!), but if you're willing to set your search radius wider or if you have your heart set on a specific breed, many places have an active online presence. Animal shelter social media accounts have endless cute pics of unhoused hounds. As you scroll, be aware that the heart-wrenching stories designed to make you fill out an adoption application can trigger a tear or two. (Cue Sarah McLachlan singing "In the arms of the angel . . .")

BREEDERS

Widespread spay and neuter policies have reduced the number of unwanted litters, which means many areas have too few dogs for the adoption market demand. If you find yourself in this position, you may choose to purchase a dog.

Pet stores typically rely on mass breeding facilities known as puppy mills, which are crowded and unsanitary, and they don't screen for health issues. So if you decide to buy a dog, skip the pet stores and find an ethical breeder. Some breeders have only a few dogs that produce a small number of litters every year, and they make the best efforts to ensure the pups are happy and healthy. Choosing the right breeder is all about doing your due doggy diligence because there isn't a perfect directory that lets you easily find a reputable source. Signs of a responsible breeder include years of experience and willingness to bring the receipts. The documents you should expect from a legit breeder include a contract for sale, a registration certificate, an ID tag, a full medical history, including vaccination certificates, and breeding records. When you visit the facility in person, it's a good sign if the mother is present and interacting with her babies. Don't settle for less before you settle down.

FOSTERING

If you're not ready for a long-term commitment but want to dip your toes in the water bowl, fostering is a great way to care for a dog for a few days, weeks, or months. Many shelters at full capacity rely on foster parents to provide temporary homes. Fostering doesn't have to be a one-night stand, either. Fostering to adopt is a common way for people to test out compatibility before they say "I do" and their dog says "I awooooooooo."

Setting Your Age Range

Do you like 'em young, or do you want a silver fox-(hound)? Although age is just a number, it can make all the difference—especially when those numbers are multiplied in dog years! When you're looking for a canine companion, think about what stage they're at in life—and what stage you're at, too. Keeping these things in mind can help keep both of you happy for years to come.

PUPPIES

Oh so cute, but oh so much work—and money! The first years of a dog's life are a critical time in their development, so you'll need the best quality food you can afford to ensure your little one grows healthy and strong. The American Kennel Club suggests that puppies get at least three square meals a day. Try to fight the urge to feed them table scraps. Begging for food is a hard habit to break!

When it comes to accessories, an adjustable collar and leash are best because pups grow fast. A heating pad that is pet safe is a comforting accessory that can mimic the warmth and closeness of littermates. Finally, one of the most important things you'll need is a training plan. It takes a lot of time and specific gear to housebreak a puppy. You may want to find a trainer or attend a class to show you the ropes.

ADULTS

If you'd like to bypass the puppy stage, consider looking for a partner with a bit more life experience. While that uncontrollable puppy energy may wear off after a year or two, moving into a new home can still be stressful for a more mature mutt and cause them to act out. Even if you rescue an adult from an undesirable environment, that setting was filled with familiar sights and smells. Make them feel safe and secure as they transition into their new life by establishing a routine.

It also helps to designate a small, controlled area in the beginning. Pet gates, pens, or crates can create a safe haven during the adjustment period. The best mindset for dealing with an adult rescue is to treat them like a puppy. Assume they haven't been trained and be ready to deal with cheeky behavior or naughty habits they may have picked up.

SENIORS

Everyone deserves to be loved, no matter their age or background. This is especially true for older pooches and great-great-granddogs. The plus side is that you *can* teach an old dog new tricks. It may even be easier than with a puppy because they're much more chill and have a better attention span.

Senior pet care is all about focusing on health and mobility. Hardwood floors and tiles can be slippery for seniors, so covering these areas with rugs or mats is helpful. Depending on the dog, your home or car may need pet steps, ramps, lifting harnesses, and extra dog blankets to keep Really Old Yeller as comfy as possible. Just like humans, joint pain and weakened muscles are a reality of old age for graying greyhounds, aging affenpinschers, and every other oldie. Some dogs may need special food, supplements, and multivitamins. Veterans need veterinarians, so establish a good relationship with a vet. Regular checkups will ensure happiness in their twilight years.

The Doggy Dating Scene

You've figured out what you want and where to find it. Now what? Just like in the human world, every experience will depend on where you go, what you're looking for, and who you meet. But there are some fairly standard parts of the process.

Make the first move. After you've made a connection, there will be an application process. The adoption market can be highly competitive, so you may have to provide extensive information about your reasons for adopting, your home and financial situation, and your experience with animals. This can feel invasive, but it's no time to be shy or coy—playing hard to get will make it hard to get a dog. Due to high demand, many places won't be able to respond right away. They may even ghost you. Begging is usually something dogs do, but at this stage, it's humans who are doing the begging.

The first date. Whether you've found your potential match online or fallen in love at first sight IRL, the initial meet and greet may happen before or after the application process. Whichever order you do it, the first date is an opportunity to see if you feel the spark with Sparky.

Picking up the tab. There's no debate about splitting the bill. Purchasing from a breeder can set you back thousands of dollars, and shelters and rescues generally charge an adoption fee, which covers spaying/neutering, microchips, and initial medical care, so it's worth it.

The Cohabitation Starter Pack

"Wanna come back to my place?" You made a match and you're ready to make it official! Now you'll need to offer your date a ride to their forever home. Make sure you have an appropriate carrier that fits the size of your pup or a seatbelt harness for safe transportation.

Moving in together is a huge step for humans and hounds alike. When you bring home your new love, there will be an adjustment period that can take weeks or months. Hang in there! Like a basset hound's droopy ears or a bulldog's slobbery jowls, keep hanging. And be sure to consider these tips for a smooth transition.

Make sure your place is pet-proofed before those furry four legs walk through the front door. Get down on all fours and remove any potential hazards: Hide electrical cords as best you can, lock cabinets with food or toxic chemicals, keep houseplants up high, and move small chewable items like shoes and laundry out of reach.

When you get home, be patient as your pup gets familiar with their new surroundings, new family, and new routine. Part of that routine will involve training: potty training, basic commands like "sit" and "stay," and leash walking are just a few lessons you may need to teach.

You don't need an Edible Arrangement to greet your dog, but you should have basic supplies ready and available. Start with dog food, food and water bowls, a collar and leash, poop bags, a dog bed, treats and toys, and grooming supplies like a brush and nail trimmers.

Ready to meet your match?

Turn the page to flip through a diverse directory of delight-ful doggos. As you paw through the profiles, remember that they are totally tongue-in-cheek. These fun, silly snapshots are generalizations of pooch personalities. Just like people, dogs are individuals. You can't create a complete picture of yourself when you make a dating profile, and the same is true for dogs.

We've consulted the American Kennel Club (akc.org) to get the deets on dog breeds, and although some of the physi-cal traits you'll find in the profiles, like size and shedding, are more predictable, not all dogs of the same breed will have the same temperament and behavior. Much of that is shaped by how they're raised and how they're trained. That's where you come in!

Start swiping!

The Bare Bones

Each pup profile has the following labels to help you find your match. And if you already know what you're looking for, there's also a Quick Rufference Guide on page 108 that lists dogs by size, amount of shedding, barking habits, and more.

 These stats use the median weight and height of each dog breed. Keep in mind that in most cases, a female dog will be smaller than their male counterparts.

EXTRA-SMALL: Dogs between 5 and 10 inches in height that weigh between 3 and 15 pounds.

SMALL: Dogs between 8 and 15 inches in height that weigh between 12 and 30 pounds.

MEDIUM: Dogs between 14 and 25 inches in height that weigh between 35 and 70 pounds.

LARGE: Dogs between 21 and 30 inches in height that weigh between 50 and 100 pounds.

EXTRA-LARGE: Dogs that are over 26 inches in height that weigh more than 110 pounds.

 With regular checkups and proper care, most dog breeds will live to be at least 10 years old. However, genetics will always factor into your pup's lifespan.

 Will your lint roller become a permanent appendage? This will help you know whether to stock up.

 See if you're looking at a couch pup-tato or a dog with a perpetual case of the zoomies.

 In addition to being good with children, this icon takes into consideration a dog's openness to strangers and their ability to adapt to new situations.

Brussels Griffon
QUIRKY CUTIE

EXTRA-SMALL	12 TO 15 YEARS	LOW	MEDIUM	3 / 5

One look at me and you might think my name should be Brussels Gremlin. I have a funny little face that makes me look more like an Ewok from *Star Wars* than a run-of-the-mill hound. But that's part of my charm! I'm not quite a toy and I'm not quite a terrier, but I'm quite the character. Griffs are little dogs who are a little eccentric, so let's get silly!

My ideal first date
Let's check out a comedy show. I'll be the comic relief, with my high-spirited, curious, and spunky behavior. I'm mischievous, but I'll always let you in on the joke.

It might surprise you that
I get along well with cats! If you have a feline friend, that's cool with me. Kids, on the other hand, can be a bit too much for my small stature and sensitive nature, unless they're not prone to roughhousing.

We'll get along if
You don't need much personal space. I'm a Velcro dog, which means I'm super clingy. All I want is to be with my family, so I tend to stick close. Who said codependent relationships were a bad thing?!

Labrador Retriever
AT YOUR SERVICE

LARGE | 12 TO 14 YEARS | HIGH | HIGH | 5 / 5

Hello, friend! Is this your first time? If so, that's okay! I'm good-natured and easy to train—the perfect pooch for those new to the puppy scene. I'm a quick study who graduated top of my class in obedience school. While I might consider my options as a therapy dog or service dog, I'm happy be your loyal sidekick or friendliest, furriest family member.

The award I should be nominated for
Most Popular Pup. Did you know I'm the most popular breed in America?

Don't hate me if
I search your closet for my solemate. I've been known to chew up a shoe or ten. It's in my blood (and my name). As a retriever, I'm used to retrieving things, and without apposable thumbs, I have to use my mouth. Invest in some quality chew toys to keep me away from your things.

An overshare
You'll find out soon enough, but I can't stop and won't stop shedding. I lose hair year-round, and twice a year I have bonus seasonal shedding! My stiff hairs wind up everywhere, so a lint roller will be your new go-to accessory. I think it's a small price to pay for my never-ending affection and companionship.

Irish Setter
HAIR GOALS

LARGE | 12 TO 15 YEARS | MEDIUM | HIGH | 5 / 5

If you've got a thing for leggy redheads, then the luck of the Irish is with you today. My glossy, feathered, mahogany coat is as gorgeous as my personality is sweet. I'm friendly, outgoing, and up for anything—especially anything sporty. I have a lot of energy to burn, so I love to keep active. Let's run a lap (or 20) around the block together!

I get distracted by
Sights! Sounds! Smells! People! Places! Yes, I'm impulsive, but with some obedience training, I easily develop the good manners and grace befitting my appearance.

Favorite movie genre
Anything G-rated. All ages are admitted to experience my affection and friendship. I'm a family-friendly dog who is good-natured around everyone, including other animals.

I can be a bit
High maintenance. This chestnut hair doesn't stay luxurious on its own. You'll be brushing me several times a week to maintain these Pantene-commercial locks.

My theme song is
"One Is the Loneliest Number." I'm a happy and positive pooch, but I get separation anxiety, so please don't leave me alone all day!

Basset Hound
LOW-KEY & LOW-PROFILE

| MEDIUM | 12 TO 13 YEARS | MEDIUM | MEDIUM | 4 / 5 |

Elvis accused my breed of being "nothin' but a hound dog," but what does he know? I refuse to take the words of a man who wore a rhinestone jumpsuit to heart. Sometimes, I refuse to take orders, period. But even if I'm not the biggest people-pleaser, I'm calm and easy-going. That's why I'm great around kids, strangers, and other animals.

Best vacation memory
The thing is, I go on a lot of trips. My long ears are literally a tripping hazard. I've been known to stumble over them, especially as a puppy.

I need a partner who
Takes things one step at a time. Have you seen my legs? These little stumps have trouble going up and down stairs, so I'm best suited to a single-story home or an elevator building.

Don't hate me if
I screen your calls. I was bred to track scents, so it's in my nature to completely ignore you as I wander off to investigate an intriguing smell.

My favorite time of day is
Nap time! (Which is most of the day.)

Boston Terrier
DRESSED TO IMPRESS

SMALL

11 TO 13
YEARS

LOW

MEDIUM

4 / 5

Are you new to this? Don't be nervous! I'm the pawfect pooch for new pup parents. If this is your first time with a fur baby, you're in good paws. I'm friendly, loyal, and very smart, which means I'm receptive to training. If you teach me a thing or two, I'll teach you how much fun it is to have a dog in your life!

My star sign is
A Libra. The balanced scales perfectly represent my personality: I'm not too active but not too lazy, either. Playtime and exercise are just as important to me as relaxing.

My biggest failure is
Because I love people so much, I can get overexcited and deliver super sloppy kisses. My mouthy nature isn't always loved by younger kids and strangers, but many find my snoring, snorting, and slobbering very endearing.

My must-have accessory
Like my "tuxedo coat"? That's all me, baby! Like any dapper fellow, I'm always dressed to impress, and I have impeccable manners to match, which have earned me the nickname of the "American Gentleman."

Dalmatian
101 REASONS TO LOVE

MEDIUM   11 TO 13 YEARS   MEDIUM   HIGH   3 / 5

I attract a lot of attention when I'm strutting my stuff, so get used to being in the *spot*light when I'm by your side. You'll also have to get used to keeping up with me when I'm by your side. I have a LOT of energy I need to burn, and there's nothing I love more than running, roaming, and staying active.

A trait I inherited

I have an outgoing personality and I'm friendly, but I can be wary—and even a little aggressive— toward strangers. My kind were bred as guard dogs back in the day, and I still embody the protective tendencies of my ancestors unless I'm socialized to new people and places from a very young age.

How to keep the spark alive

When you've been with someone for a long time, it can be difficult to keep things exciting. Because I have so much energy, I get bored really easily. I'll need lots of toys, lots of space, and lots of attention to keep me stimulated and prevent me from getting destructive.

We probably won't get along if

You're a homebody. If we're not moving, we're not living!

Rottweiler
LARGE & IN CHARGE

| LARGE | 9 TO 10 YEARS | HIGH | HIGH | 3 / 5 |

If you're looking for a strong, confident guardian, look no farther. As a born-and-bred guard dog, I'm a fierce protector of those I love. But when it comes to relationships, I like to take it slow. I prefer to stand back and read the room before I let anyone in—into my home and into my heart.

My mantra is
"Let's get ready to (g)rumble!" When I sense a threat, I have a deep, intimidating growl. But the sound you'll hear from me most often is my "rumble"—that's the thick, grumbly purring I make when I get belly rubs!

My signature move is
The "Rottie Lean." I may be big and mighty, but I have the tendencies of a lap dog. I love to get up close and personal and will lean my full weight against you. Since I can weigh up to 135 pounds, you might want to focus on strength training the next time you hit the gym.

You might be surprised to learn
I may look like another dumb jock, but I've got serious brain power. I can master new tricks easily, which makes me a great service dog.

American Pit Bull Terrier

SWEET SWOLEMATE

| MEDIUM | 12 TO 14 YEARS | LOW | HIGH | 4 / 5 |

It's nice to meet you, new friend! I'm super sweet, super intelligent, and super strong. That strength has contributed to some bad PR (Pit bull Relations), and I've gained an unfair reputation as a "bad dog" in recent years. But all I need is a lot of love and a little help to reach my best potential—just like other dogs and, let's face it, people!

My ideal partner
Someone with confidence and time to properly train and socialize me. When you put in the work, I'm an affectionate companion who gets along with everyone. I'm people-friendly and I really adore kids! Whether you're a party of one or a full-house family, I'll fit right in.

Something you can't tell by my photos
I'm as intelligent as I am athletic. My smarts and stamina make me a great service dog or therapy dog.

Celebrity doppelgänger
This old-school reference is a bit of a deep cut, but have you ever seen *The Little Rascals*? It's about a bunch of neighborhood kids who hang out with a pit bull named Petey. I'm totally Petey. I told you I love kids!

English Bulldog
CHUNKY & CHARMING

| MEDIUM | 8 TO 10 YEARS | LOW | LOW | 5 / 5 |

Brumff! For those of you who don't speak Bulldog, that is my standard greeting snort. My short squishy muzzle makes a lot of unique noises. If you put grumbling, snorting, sniffling, and chortling in a blender, you'd be playing the song of my people. Speaking of people, there's few I don't get along with. I love kids! I love adults! I love attention! And if you give me some attention, you'll get a sloppy, slobbery kiss in return.

You might be surprised to learn
Despite my intimidating looks, I am truly the goodest! I have a good nature, good manners, and good looks. Okay, I might not be conventionally attractive, but I'm very good-looking if your type is jowly, wrinkly, and doughy.

I love anyone who has
Air-conditioning. It doesn't take much to keep me happy, but I really do best in areas that stay comfortably cool. I overheat easily.

My ideal first date
Some people like long walks on the beach, but I prefer short walks around the block. And by "walk" I mean "shuffle." A slow stroll followed by a long snooze would be truly *harrumphhbrr.* (That's Bulldog for "awesome.")

Pomeranian
READY FOR MY CLOSE-UP

 EXTRA-SMALL

12 TO 16 YEARS

MEDIUM

 LOW

3 / 5

I'm a tiny pup with BDE: Big Dog Energy. What I lack in size, I make up for in personality. This perky Pom is a foxy, feisty fur baby, and I love being the center of attention. Let's make things clear: It's my world and you're just living in it. I know my worth. If you can't handle me at my sassiest, you don't deserve me at my sweetest.

My ideal first date
A Broadway show . . . in which I'm the star! For tonight's performance, the role of everybody will be played by me! I love to put on a show, and I will keep you constantly entertained.

I'm not afraid to
Speak up! I have a shrill voice and I demand to be heard. This makes me an excellent watchdog, but not the best match if your place is a quiet zone.

Biggest turn-off
Little kids. If you've got tiny tots, call me back in ten years. I'm much better around adults and older children. Although I'm a toy dog breed, I don't want to be treated like an actual toy by small children.

Shar-Pei
ROLLS ON ROLLS ON ROLLS

MEDIUM   8 TO 12 YEARS   LOW   MEDIUM   3 / 5

Excuse me, what are you looking at? I may have a unique appearance that attracts a lot of attention, but I do *not* warm up to strangers very easily. I'm downright icy, aloof, and suspicious of anyone outside my family. My personality is as prickly as my skin. The name shar-pei translates to "sand skin" because my coat has a sandpaper-like texture. I'm totally one-of-a-kind, and if you're the same, I'll be a calm, loyal friend.

A hot take
Is it just me or are other dogs totally cringe? All that people-pleasing and tail-wagging, all that bounding and playing. No thank you. I keep my head held high and have a quiet, regal, reserved composure.

A motto I live by
"Everything in moderation." Are you sick of the highs and lows of roller-coaster relationships? Then you should consider taking me home. I'm naturally clean, easy to housebreak, and all I need is moderate exercise.

A trend I can't get behind
Botox. Are you telling me that humans are trying to remove wrinkles? Make it make sense! I find abundant folds of skin to be very appealing, if I do say so myself.

Bernese Mountain Dog

FEEL THE BERN

LARGE | 7 TO 10 YEARS | HIGH | MEDIUM | 4 / 5

Bred in the Swiss mountains of Bern (I know, my name is incredibly uncreative), I'm looking for someone who prioritizes work-life balance the same way I do. Although I'm strong and love working outdoors, I'm no workaholic. I'm just as happy lazing around as running around. I'm totally chill in every sense of the world. Not only am I cool, calm, and collected, but I also thrive in cold environments. My thick coat is basically insulation—sorry in advance for all the shedding.

Ideal Sunday Funday
Romping around in the snow. Bring the kids, too! I'm great with little ones and will happily pull them along on their sleds.

All I ask is that you
Take things slow. I'm very reserved, especially around people I don't know. I'm looking for someone to socialize me and bring me out of my shell. When that happens, I'll be your perfect pal!

Something you'll never see me do
Be aggressive. I may be large and powerful, but I'm not mean or aggro. I'm a pacifist—I am Swiss, after all!

French Bulldog
NETFLIX & NUZZLES

SMALL | 10 TO 12 YEARS | LOW | LOW | 5 / 5

Bonjour! I'm a bite-sized bulldog with a smiley smush face. I'd be the pawfect pal for a city dweller who wants a cuddle buddy. Small apartments are my kind of home. (A big doghouse? In this economy?) Plus, I rarely bark, so you'll never have to deal with passive-aggressive noise complaints from the grumpy guy who lives down the hall.

My ideal first date
A very leisurely walk around the block. Do you only have the time and energy for short walks? Me too! My little legs and flat face make me run out of breath easily, so I prefer casual strolls around the neighborhood over high-octane physical activities.

You'll have to get used to
Blaming the dog. Frenchies are flatulent and we toot all day long. If the foul stench of frequent farting is a deal breaker, I might not be the pooch for you.

My attachment style
Although I'm easygoing, I get really attached to my family, so I can get pretty anxious if you leave me alone for too long.

Australian Shepherd
RUFF & TUMBLE

MEDIUM | 12 TO 15 YEARS | HIGH | HIGH | 3 / 5

Wowgreattomeetyoudoyouwannaplayfetch?!?! Or we could play Frisbee, go for a hike, and race around the dog park—all before breakfast! Are you getting exhausted just reading that? I'm not! Let's goooooo!

My party trick
Do I have to pick one? I have a ton of tricks up my silky sleeve! I'm super smart and agile, so you can teach me complex commands. Sit? Stay? Yawn. I could do the entire choreography from Beyoncé's "Single Ladies" while balancing a ball on my head.

My best feature
The eyes have it! I'm known for my steely, penetrating stare, especially when I'm hyper-focused on something.

My most irrational fear
Losing one of the flock. I'm a herding dog, so I love rounding up cattle and sheep. But if you don't live on a ranch, I'll just keep you in line instead. Watch your feet because I'm not above nipping at your heels.

Samoyed
SAY CHEESE!

| MEDIUM | 12 TO 14 YEARS | HIGH | HIGH | 4 / 5 |

What's got me smiling from fluffy ear to fluffy ear? Honestly, I don't even know! I have a naturally upturned mouth, so I'm always grinning. I guess you could call it resting happy face. What truly makes me happy, though, is frolicking through the snow. If you're a ski bunny or snow bro, we're bound to have a ton of fun.

How I'll get your attention
It's not so much how I'll get your attention, but *howl* I'll get your attention. My communication style involves a lot of barking and distinctive whining. If you can't handle the noise, we're probably not a match.

My hobbies include
Sledding and shedding. I have a thick double coat that's made for snowy, cold climates. It's also made for excessive shedding. Lint rollers and a heavy-duty vacuum cleaner will be your new best friends. Well, second and third best friends, after me!

I relax by
I know the hair seems like a lot, but it also makes for the softest snuggles! I'm a big-time cuddler who will keep you warm and cozy on winter nights.

Greyhound
LESS RACING, MORE RELAXING

| LARGE | 10 TO 13 YEARS | LOW | LOW | 5 / 5 |

Although I'm best known for my skills as a track star—I can get up to 45 miles per hour—I'm actually laidback, low maintenance, and a little lazy. If you let me, I'll sleep up to 22 hours a day! I'm like a tall, skinny housecat.

What I'm looking for
Anything? Everything? No, really. I have a 270-degree range of vision, so I can see objects behind me and over half a mile in front of me. And I'm a sighthound, so if I see something fun, like squirrels or rabbits, I'm on the chase. I'll leave other dogs, kids, and babies alone, though. In fact, I'm so gentle, I'm perfect for families with little ones.

Things I won't do
Barking and shedding. Well, only a little. I'm quiet, clean, and great for first-time pup parents. I told you I was low maintenance!

I want someone who
Keeps their voice down. I'm a bit sensitive and get anxious around loud noises.

Something you can't tell by my photos
Out of all purebred dog breeds, I'm known to have the least amount of hereditary health issues.

Labradoodle
HAPPIEST HYBRID

MEDIUM	12 TO 15 YEARS	LOW	HIGH	4 / 5

The sweetness of a labrador and the smarts of a poodle—get you a dog who does both! I'm a crossbred cutie (also known as a "designer dog") designed to live with people who have allergies, which means my curly coat doesn't shed as much as other pooches. Medical disclaimer voice: "Consult your human doctor if you have allergies before you bring me home."

I want someone who
Has as much energy as me! I'm a high-key hybrid who needs to run around in open spaces. If I get bored or am trapped inside for too long, I can get a little destructive. Don't worry—I'm still gentle and affectionate . . . just not with any shoes or fun things you might leave around.

I'm a regular at
The beach. Or the lake. Or the pool. I'm a fantastic swimmer and I love being in the water.

I bring new meaning to the phrase
"Friends with benefits." I'm really eager to be friends with everyone, and the benefit is that I'm lots of fun!

German Shepherd
SERVE & PROTECT

 LARGE   12 TO 14 YEARS   HIGH   HIGH   4 / 5

Officer K9, reporting for duty! I'm a workaholic watchdog who's at my best when tackling tasks and challenges. I require a lot of training, but with positive reinforcement and patience, I'll be your fearless friend till the end.

This year, I really want to
Get physical. Long walks? Long runs? Long play sessions? I'm longing for all of it! I require a lot of daily exercise, and I'm looking for someone who needs the same.

Believe it or not . . .
I'm a big softie with a silly side. I've heard that I can seem intimidating, but it's just that I take my job very seriously. When I'm off the clock, I love to play and cuddle and spend time with my family, just like the next dog. If I've grown up around humans and other animals, I'm an amazing team player.

Don't be jealous if
You catch me checking out strangers. I'm sizing people up to see if I can take them in a fight. It's just an occupational hazard for a guard dog like myself, not a sign of disloyalty.

Cocker Spaniel
SWEET & STURDY

SMALL	10 TO 14 YEARS	HIGH	MEDIUM	4 / 5

With my big dewy eyes, long lashes, and sweet expression, you might think I'm a dainty creature. Although I'm gentle and loving, I'm tougher than people take me for. I was bred as a hunting dog, so I'm as comfortable in nature as I am on the couch. However, if you're looking for a guard dog, I'm more likely to greet intruders with excessive wagging than excessive force.

We'll get along if
I'm an easygoing pup, but my silky, flowing coat needs a lot of attention. If you're not put off by frequent grooming, brushing, clipping, and trimming to keep me detangled and looking darling, we'll be BFFs.

Best travel story
As my name suggests, I'm originally from Spain, but breed lore has it that one of my ancestors came over to America from England on the *Mayflower*. This means there are both English and American cocker spaniels with different traits. American tend to be smaller, with rounder heads, and English have longer snouts and less impressive brows.

Together we could . . .
Do everything, please? Sorry, but I need a lot of PDA and can become a bit vocal if I'm left alone. Good thing I'm incredibly smart and can learn enough tricks to keep us entertained.

Chow Chow
CANINE KING

| MEDIUM | 8 TO 12 YEARS | HIGH | MEDIUM | 2 / 5 |

Behold me, the magnificent chow chow, in all my glory! Bow down to my blue-black tongue when I bowwow! Admire my majestic mane! The lion is the king of the jungle, but I'm the royalty of the canine kingdom. I wish—no, I *demand*—to have the finest creature comforts. If you want to join me in the lap of luxury, you'll have to earn my trust and respect.

The hallmark of a good relationship is
Exclusivity. I'm not here to see other people. Frankly, I'm wary and suspicious of most people, but those in my inner circle will be rewarded with the utmost loyalty. Without proper training, I can get aggressive around those I don't know, including other pets and small children.

One thing I'll never do again
Go swimming. My amazing coat may look good, but it's heavy when it gets wet and results in some subpar dog-paddling.

My nickname is
I've been called "Cat Dog." I'm clean, quiet, stubborn, and a bit fussy. I'm not fond of being held or cuddled. Affection? I've never heard of her. I don't understand how other dogs are so . . . needy. Have they no dignity?

Pug
DTS: DOWN TO SNUGGLE

SMALL	13 TO 15 YEARS	MEDIUM	LOW	4 / 5

Need a lovable low-key lapdog who lives to laze? Stop looking! I'm right here! No, down here—I'm a barely a foot tall, so please watch your step. My love of naps doesn't mean my personality is a snooze, though. When I'm awake, I'm happy and excitable. Just don't get me too worked up, because I'm brachycephalic. That's a fancy human word for "flat, wrinkled face that's super adorable." (I may or may not have added that last part.) Since my face makes me susceptible to breathing problems, I'm best suited to minimal physical activity. Indoor kids, unite!

My favorite pastime
Cuddling or napping. Right now, the latter sounds especially appealing because I just had a five-minute walk. Mmm, I'm just gonna settle down here and . . . zzzzzzzzzzzzzzzzzzzz

A social cause I care about
Zzzzzzzzzzzzzzzzzzzzzzzzzzzzzzzzzzzzzzzzz

Let's debate this topic
Zzzzzzzzzzzzzzzzzzzzzzzzzzzzzzzzzzzzzzzzz

Let me treat you to this
. . . Did you say "treat"?! I'm awake! I was just resting my eyes, I swear.

Siberian Husky

5-ALARM HOWLER

MEDIUM   12 TO 14 YEARS   HIGH   HIGH   5 / 5

I'm a friendly, happy hound who needs a confident parent. I easily adapt to new situations, but I'm as independent as I am intelligent and easygoing, so I can be pretty difficult to train. If you're a pup owner who's been around the block (on dog walks) or can give me the consistent training I need, we'll be friends furever!

My ideal first date

An escape room. I love exploring and don't like to be left alone, so if you keep me somewhere for too long I'll find a way out. Call me Houdini—I'm a world-class escape artist.

I'm big on

Communication. And I mean BIG—my wolflike howling can go on for hours. Maybe call me *Howl*dini instead.

You might be surprised to learn

Despite my intimidating wolfy looks, I am a goofy, playful, social butterfly. Strangers? Friends I haven't met yet! Kids? Love 'em! Other pets? The bigger the pack, the better!

My karaoke song is

"AAROWROWWOWWOWAHWAW (the extended cut)"

German Shorthaired Pointer

BORN 2 HUNT

MEDIUM   10 TO 12 YEARS   MEDIUM   HIGH   4 / 5

Are you looking for an all-star athlete who is alert, agile, and active? Then look no farther! I'm an outdoorsy jock who wants to hang out and play games with you. I won't be playing games with your heart, though, because I'm loyal, loving, and family-friendly. As a hunting dog, it's in my nature to keep a close eye (and nose) on everything around me. I get easily distracted if I catch an interesting sight or smell and— What was that? Did you see that? I'm picking up a scent! EXCUSE ME, I MUST INVESTIGATE.

Pet peeves

If you like to sleep in on Sundays, spend hours inside curled up with a book, and don't have an active lifestyle, then swipe to the next pup profile. And maybe consider getting a cat instead.

My secret talent

I'm such a hardworking dog that I have an extra side hustle: modeling. Maybe you've seen me in a Ralph Lauren or L.L.Bean ad? My "blue steel" is a dignified gaze into the middle distance while I stand on a dock beside a man who is wearing a cable-knit sweater. I might be of German descent, but my vibe is classic all-American.

Cavalier King Charles Spaniel

BFF: BEST FRIENDS FUREVER

SMALL	12 TO 15 YEARS	MEDIUM	LOW	5 / 5

Yes, my name has a royal title in it, but don't worry! I promise I'm just as comfortable on the couch as I am on the throne. My size and expressive eyes might give me the look of a toy, but I've got the outdoorsy instincts of a spaniel in my blood, and I love to run and play before taking a nice nap on your lap. I'm a pint-sized pup that contains multitudes!

Award I should be nominated for

Most popular. I'll strike up conversation with everyone we meet on our walks. I'll even become besties with kids, cats, and other pets.

My best feature

Hmmm . . . just one? Although I'm sure you'll love my silky coat (or I hope you will because you'll need to brush it often), I'd have to go with my eyes. These textbook puppy-dog peepers can always get me out of the trouble I get into when my stubborn nature surfaces and I refuse to listen to you. Seriously, how can you stay mad at this face?

My order for the table

One of everything! I'll overindulge when it comes to food, so you'll need to keep an eye on my diet and walk me every day.

Shiba Inu

AFFECTIONATE & FOXY

SMALL | 13 TO 16 YEARS | MEDIUM | MEDIUM | 2 / 5

Are you up for a challenge? I'm a small dog with the cunning—and looks!—of a sly fox. I'm here to outwit you, outrun you, and generally just get into mischief. But if you can put up with my antics, I'll reward you with all my love and affection. (And how could you not? Have you seen how cute I am?)

We'll get along if
You're a neat freak who likes alone time. I've been told I'm more like a cat than a dog, especially when it comes to my personal hygiene and need for "me time."

Most spontaneous thing I've done
I need mental and physical stimulation, so if given the chance to do, well, anything, I'm going to take it. I love exploring, digging, and playing, and when combined with my confidence, my curiosity can get me into trouble—so make sure to keep an eye on me when we're out and about.

I am a huge fan of
Saying how you feel. If I'm unhappy, I'll let you know—and everyone else, too. The Shiba Scream has been known to haunt groomers, dog walkers, and unsuspecting bystanders around the globe.

Golden Retriever

EAGER 2 PLEASE

 LARGE   10 TO 12 YEARS   HIGH   HIGH   5 / 5

Hello! Hi! Hiiiiiiiiii!!!!! I'm REALLY EXCITED to meet you! And your family! Can I please meet your family? For real though, I know it's not cool to have no chill, so beneath my big, bro-y personality, you'll find a quiet, cuddle-loving pup who's up for anything and easy to train.

Three words to describe me
DTF: Down to Fetch. I'm a retriever after all!

Never have I ever
Met someone I didn't like. I'm a people-pleasing pup who gets along with everyone! I'm especially great with kids because I'm just a big kid myself—my sweet, silly puppy energy stays with me into my adult years.

My karaoke song
"You've Got a Friend in Me"

You should not message me if
You've got a super sensitive sniffer. I have a very distinct doggy odor, and you'll need a high tolerance for *eau de retriever* if we're going to be spending all our time together.

Beagle
CHEERFUL & CHEEKY

SMALL | 10 TO 15 YEARS | LOW | HIGH | 4 / 5

I'm smart and strong-willed, so I like to be stimulated with plenty of exercise, tasks, and jobs. When Rihanna sang "work, work, work, work, work, work," I really felt that. And when I feel something, I will let you know. A simple bark when there's someone at the door, sure, but if I'm super excited or feel left out, I've got two separate sets of howls to get your attention. I wear my heart on my snout.

My best pickup line
"What scent are you wearing?" Seriously. I'm driven by scents and smells, and my floppy ears actually help me pick up a scent.

I'm curious about
Everything! I'm an inquisitive, mischievous dog who will sniff my way into all kinds of adventures if you don't keep me entertained.

My friends call me
"Goldilocks." I'm not aggressive, but I'm not shy. I'm friendly but not clingy. I'm energetic, but I love to lay around, too. I'm juuuust right.

Chihuahua
SWEET & SPICY

EXTRA-SMALL	14 TO 16 YEARS	LOW	LOW	2 / 5

I'm extra small, extra cute, and just plain extra. I'm sweet, silly, and sassy. Some might even say I can be a real spoiled brat, especially if I'm not trained. If you're interested in getting to know me, let's talk. Well, I'll be doing all the talking. I'm a very vocal pooch who is prone to long, loud barking.

My ideal working conditions
Work from home works for me! I can get into trouble if I'm left unsupervised, plus I crave attention and constant companionship, so I'd be perfect for someone who spends a lot of time around the home.

Dream vacation
Anywhere warm! And since life is a vacation for me, I'd prefer to live in a warm climate. I get cold very easily, so I'll need lots of warm layers if we're anywhere chilly. On the plus side, think of how cute those tiiiiiny sweaters will look on me.

You might be surprised to learn
I'm a serial monogamist. Look, I know what I like. I have a tendency to bond with one person, and if that person is you, we'll be snuggling and cuddling all day long! But if you're prone to jealousy, you should get a golden retriever or something.

Airedale Terrier
GIFTED & TALENTED

| MEDIUM | 11 TO 14 YEARS | LOW | MEDIUM | 3 / 5 |

Good day to you! I'm an overachiever who is the opposite of an underdog. I'm dignified, intelligent, courageous, and athletic. Don't be intimidated, though. I'm not a pretentious, pampered pup. I'm friendly, polite, and don't require much grooming. I bet when you see how expertly I catch a ball, you'll catch feelings.

My most annoying personality trait
Unless you show me otherwise, I'll be convinced I'm the one in charge. My enthusiasm, energy, and smarts make me headstrong. I'll always be top dog, but you should assert your dominance so I don't micromanage you.

I bet you can't
Find something I'm not good at! Military dog, police dog, presidential sidekick, search-and-rescue dog, therapy dog, agility dog, hunting dog—I've done it all. I can thrive in apartments and houses, and my coat is adaptable to all kinds of weather. With so much versatility in my paws, can't you see why I think I'm the boss?

Red flags
Cats. Unless you socialize me to feline friends at a very young age, I have a hard time mixing with kitties. My hunting instincts kick in when I'm around them, and I can't help but chase and get rambunctious.

Great Dane

GENTLE GIANT

EXTRA-LARGE	7 TO 10 YEARS	MEDIUM	MEDIUM	4 / 5

It seems like everyone is lying about their height on their profile. But believe me, there's no *dog*fishing going on here. When I stand on my hind legs, I'm taller than most people. But there's so much more to me than that. I'm a gentle, patient, affectionate creature who is easygoing and mild-mannered.

I have a reputation for

Being a homewrecker. No, I'm not here to break up your marriage. But I might break your wedding china. When I lumber through your home, things will get knocked off tables and shelves. Despite this, I'm perfectly comfortable in small homes and apartments. You just need to make sure I have enough space to move around without damaging your stuff.

I'm all about

That bass. My voice is so deep that you could call me a subwoofer. Some people get intimidated when I hit those low notes, but my bark is much worse than my bite. In fact, I don't even have a bite to speak of—I'm not naturally aggressive, and I can even be a little shy.

My favorite TV show is

Scooby-Doo. A talking Great Dane who solves mysteries? Name a more beautiful work of staggering genius. I'll wait.

Boxer

STRONG, SENSITIVE & SLOBBERY

LARGE	10 TO 12 YEARS	LOW	HIGH	3 / 5

I may look serious and swole but don't be intimidated by my strong build and sleek muscles. I'm more of a class clown than a class act. And I definitely wasn't the class valedictorian. I'm rowdy and rambunctious, so it takes a lot of time and energy to train me. But if you can get this derpy doofus under control, I'll be the most fun and loyal buddy you ever had!

My ideal first date
Let's set up a zoom meeting. No, not a video chat. (Haven't you had enough of those?) I'm prone to getting the zoomies, so let's go to a big park where I can race around and stretch my long legs.

Musician I relate to
Drake. Truth be told, I'm a sensitive pup who gets really caught up in my feelings. Be warned: I will whimper and make sad eyes whenever you discipline me. As far as I'm concerned, the word "emo" is short for "emotional" and "emotionally manipulative."

We'll get along if
You can put up with snorting, wheezing, slobbering, and drooling.

Corgi
SWEET SHORT STACK

| SMALL | 12 TO 13 YEARS | HIGH | HIGH | 4 / 5 |

Live? Laugh? Love? Check, check, check! I may be small, but I've got a personality and zest for life much larger than my compact build. You might think my size is just right for cuddling, but I'm no lap dog. Who has time for naps when there's so much to do?

My greatest asset
I have my own viral hashtag: #corgibutt. So you could say my greatest ass-et is my fluffy dump truck! My posterior pouf has a distinct little waddle that has made me an Instagram influencer. You'll never want me to leave, but you'll love to watch me go.

How I handle problems
I like to nip things in the bud. You know, I just like to nip things, period. I come from a long line of cattle-herding dogs, so I'll bite at the heels of anything that moves. My bite comes with a bark, too. I'm not aggressive—just a little stubborn—but be mindful of young children and other animals around me.

We'll get along if
You believe in food-based positive reinforcement! You can easily use my love of snacks to train me out of my bad habits.

Shih Tzu
FIT FOR A QUEEN

| EXTRA-SMALL | 10 TO 18 YEARS | LOW | LOW | 4 / 5 |

I know what you're thinking: I'm a prissy princess who's a high-maintenance diva. Firstly, no. Secondly, rude! The only thing about me that requires maintenance is my luxurious silky coat. (Hey, it takes effort to look this good!) In reality, I'm a kind and sweet emotional support animal. No shade to my fellow pint-sized pooches, but I'm not like other toys: I'm much less yappy and very peaceful.

3 words that describe me
Affectionate, adorable, and agile. I'm alert, too, which makes me a surprisingly good watchdog. Let's upgrade that to a quadruple-A rating.

My biggest fear
FOMO. I'll follow you wherever you go to make sure I'm always where the action is.

I won't shut up about
Celebrity shih tzu parents. Beyoncé, Mariah Carey, and Queen Elizabeth II have all adopted shih tzus! That's three queens in total, which is not surprising since I'm descended from Chinese royalty. My ancestors were prized pets during the Ming dynasty. Shall we get together and become the royal "we"?

Old English Sheepdog
SO VERY FLOOF

LARGE **10 TO 12 YEARS** **HIGH** **HIGH** **4 / 5**

Hey there! Don't get up, let me shuffle on over and introduce myself. Look, I've even brought you some presents. My thick, shaggy coat collects a lot of stuff, and I just need a little grooming. Okay, *a lot* of grooming. But you've got three or four hours a week to spare, right? It's totally worth it for a big, shaggy friend like me.

Something I find overrated
Eye contact. I don't need to use manipulative puppy-dog eyes to make you fall for me! My peepers might be hiding under a curtain of fur, but my exuberance and friendliness shine through.

Most attractive quality
Confidence. I'm a strong-willed, independent kind of dog, so I'm best suited to an experienced pet parent who can take the lead—and take the leash. You'll need a firm grip to control my romping, bounding, playful bursts.

I respond best to
Pawsitive reinforcement. A good attitude goes a long way to training and socializing me. Then you'll find I'm really adaptable, easygoing, and affectionate.

Standard Poodle
POSH POOCH

MEDIUM	10 TO 18 YEARS	LOW	HIGH	5 / 5

Hello, darling. It's a pleasure to make your acquaintance. Allow me to introduce myself: I am a proud pup of the purest pedigree. Although I am the height of elegance and sophistication, you mustn't mistake me for a prissy poodle. I'm exceptionally friendly, supportive, and rather playful. May I formally request the pleasure of your company?

Ask me about
My education. I graduated Summa Pup Laude, and I am renowned as one of the most intelligent dog breeds. And much like those with an Ivy League education, I will never let you forget it.

A fact about me that surprises people
I'm a superior swimmer! Poodles were bred as hunting dogs, so I simply adore exercise and outdoor adventures. I am far more hardy and athletic than my polished, poofy appearance makes me seem.

My signature style is
The continental clip. This elaborate coiffure of bountiful poufs requires a fair amount of maintenance and grooming, but my curly hair is hypoallergenic. I wouldn't wish to inconvenience you with something as cumbersome as sneezing.

Bull Terrier

ENERGIZER ~~BUNNY~~ DOGGY

MEDIUM | 12 TO 13 YEARS | MEDIUM | HIGH | 3 / 5

Why the long face? If you're feeling blue, I'm here to cheer you up with my long face! My ski-slope profile and egg-shaped head aren't the only delightful things about me. I'm a happy, tail-wagging delight. If you can keep up with me, your life will be filled with fun.

I've got an appetite for

Destruction. I'm very sweet-tempered, and I don't mean any harm, but I do get bored very easily. And when I get bored, I get destructive. If you want to stop me from chewing on walls, tearing up your sofa, and excavating your yard, keep me stimulated with plenty of exercise and vigorous games, and begin training me an at early age.

My side hustle

I'm an influencer! There's a long line of spokesdogs in my history from beer-peddling Spuds Mackenzie to Bullseye, the brand ambassador for Target.

Don't be offended if

I make you repeat yourself. Bull terriers are known to be deaf or hard of hearing. Our piebald coats mean we have a low concentration of melanocytes in our inner ears which can eventually cause hearing problems.

Dachshund
SMART SAUSAGE

SMALL   12 TO 16 YEARS   LOW   MEDIUM   4 / 5

Don't let the size fool you. I might be a wee wiener, but I'm bold, brave, and brash. I'm not afraid to take on dogs much larger than me—and I often will! Although I can be a little stubborn, I'm a loyal companion and very entertaining, if I do say so myself.

My karaoke song
"(W)Hole Lotta Love." I was bred to flush out burrowing animals like badgers, so I'm prone to digging holes. (RIP your backyard.)

My dream job
Home security and surveillance operator. I'm a watchdog who is always on alert. If I see a squirrel or a person walking by, you will be the first person to hear about. Consider yourself subscribed to puppy push notifications.

My ideal first date
A game night. I thrive on puzzles, problem-solving, and intellectual challenges. Let's play hide-and-seek with my favorite treats. Or your favorite treats—I have a knack for figuring out how to steal uneaten food. Hey, was it really your snack if you let a little pooch like me escape with it?

Komondor
DREADLOCKED DOGGY

LARGE

10 TO 12 YEARS

LOW

MEDIUM

2 / 5

I'm a komondor, but there's nothing common about me. I'm a rare breed, but if you're lucky enough to meet me, you'll find a fiercely devoted and protective pal, thanks to my Hungarian herding heritage. Our relationship will take some work, but once I trust you, I'll be the most loyal mop-topped partner.

I'm looking for

An alpha dog, just like me. I'm generally calm, but not a great match for a first-time pup parent. I'm very strong-willed and unless you socialize and train me early, I can grow up to be a big pain in the tail.

Never have I ever

Owned a hairbrush. After a couple of years, I develop my signature corded locks, which don't require any brushing. But I'm not low-maintenance. My coat is a magnet for dirt and debris, and if I'm not properly dried off, I can develop a mildewy smell.

My best party trick is

Disappearing in a crowd. My crazy coat allows me to blend in with the sheep I was bred to protect. The Big Bad Wolf won't know what hit him—literally. I'll pounce on anything if I feel threatened.

Doberman Pinscher
TALL, DARK & HANDSOME

LARGE | 10 TO 12 YEARS | LOW | HIGH | 3 / 5

Want to look like a total boss with a Secret Service agent by your side? Then I'm your pup. I'm solid, sleek, muscly, and imposing. And while I'm definitely a fearless and protective guard dog, it's not always in a threatening bodyguard kinda way. The deep bond I create with people and my high intelligence make me a wonderful emotional support animal and therapy dog, if I've been trained to embrace my gentler side.

You should not go out with me if
You love a challenge. I'm all about ease. I'm easy to train and easy to groom. I'll take my eggs over-easy, too. (Just make sure I get high-quality meat and whole grains with that.)

The best kind of parties are
Cuddle parties! Under this tough exterior is a big softie. After I go for a run, all I want to do is curl up close to you.

My beauty secret is
I'm not ashamed to confess I've had a little work done. My docked tail and cropped ears have become iconic, but the practices are now illegal in most states, unless deemed medically necessary.

Miniature Schnauzer
LIFE OF THE PARTY

SMALL   12 TO 15 YEARS   LOW   MEDIUM   4 / 5

Okay everybody, let's get this party started! You might look at my salt-and-pepper hair, bushy beard, and furrowed brow and think I'm a little old gentleman, but I'm here to throw down and turn up! I need a fellow fun-seeker who wants a partner in crime for their busy, active lifestyle. If you're feisty, bright, spunky, and social, then you'll meet your match in me.

If I were a drink, I'd be
A double-shot espresso. I'm a small package that's bursting with energy and best served piping hot because I have zero chill!

My motto is
"All bark, no bite." Like many party animals, I can get pretty loud. Although my mouth can make a lot of noise, it doesn't bite. As far as I'm concerned, nipping and biting are party fouls.

My dream job
Bouncer. When you're having a blast, the last thing you need is party crashers killing the vibe. So it's a good thing I'm a little protective and can be aloof around strangers. But as soon as I understand a new person is actually your friend, they'll be totally cool with me.

Saint Bernard

DELIGHTFUL DROOL FACTORY

EXTRA-LARGE | 8 TO 10 YEARS | HIGH | MEDIUM | 5 / 5

You know those giant oversized teddy bears you can win at a carnival? That's basically me! My even-tempered personality means I'm great with kids and other animals. I do have a playful side and should probably be walked a couple times a day, but I'm mostly content to chill, nap, and lounge around. If you want a bestie or babysitter—or both!—let's make a date.

I can't live without
Hand towels. Actually, you won't be able to live without piles of towels to deal with my drool. I graduated with an MS (Master of Slobber), which means my drool flows like Niagara Falls.

My love language is
Words of af-fur-mation. I respond best to positive reinforcement. This comes in handy when you're training me. I'm well-behaved, but sometimes I don't know my own strength. Some focused sessions to curb my behavior as a pup will prevent me from bowling you and the kids over with 100+ pounds of slobbery strength and excitement.

One thing I'll never do again
Vacation in the tropics. I've got a warm and loving disposition, but bred as a cold-weather canine, I don't do well in warm climates—or even warm rooms.

Yorkshire Terrier
SMALL, SMART & SNEEZY

EXTRA-SMALL | 11 TO 15 YEARS | LOW | LOW | 4 / 5

I may be tiny, but I have a big personality—and a an even bigger mouth! I've been called a "yappy Yorkie," and I can't even be mad about it. My size makes me perfect for even the smallest home (especially if you have sound-proof walls), and I'm a great travel companion who is happy to stay by your side wherever you go.

The nerdiest thing about me
I am prone to reverse sneezing, which means that instead of pushing air out of my nose, I'll gasp for it and emit a honking sound. I'm totally fine, I swear, but I'd appreciate avoiding places with high pollen counts and other nasal annoyers.

Relationship deal breakers
Small children and other dogs. It's not just that I want to be the center of attention and get totally spoiled, it's also the fact that younger kids and bigger animals get a little too rough for my fragile frame.

My nickname is
Rapunzel. I don't shed, so without regular grooming, my hair grows into a knotted mess. For a low-maintenance mane, ask the groomer for a "puppy cut."

Pawfect Match Quiz

There's plenty of fish in the sea—

and plenty of pups in the dog park! So how do you find the one that's right for you? Let our compatibility quiz help you narrow down your options.

1. **How do you start your day?**
  a An intense workout followed by a protein shake
  b Hitting snooze and sleeping in
  c Getting the kids ready for school
  d A rich, indulgent breakfast

2. **What's your dream vacation?**
  a Hiking through the Alps
  b Relaxing on an in island in the Caribbean
  c Visiting a family-friendly amusement park
  d Clubbing and shopping in Dubai

3. What's your road trip soundtrack?

a Anything that keeps you alert and energized
b Smooth jazz and yacht rock
c Kidz Bop
d Obscure and experimental B-sides

4. Which emoji do you use most?

a Flexing bicep
b Smiley face
c Red heart
d Party cone

5. Describe your dream home.

a A sprawling ranch with plenty of outdoor space
b A charming cottage in the woods with cozy reading nooks
c A child-proofed house in the suburbs with a white picket fence
d A penthouse apartment in a major city

6. What is something you never leave home without?

a A smartwatch to track your activity throughout the day
b Noise-canceling headphones
c Goldfish crackers and Go-Gurt
d Your RSVP to an exclusive event

7. What's your go-to footwear?

a High-performance running shoes
b Comfy slippers
c Sensible sneakers
d Designer boots

MOSTLY As
Outdoor Adventurer
You work hard and play hard. And your idea of play involves intense physical activity. You need a high-octane hound who can match your energy, whether you're running an ultramarathon or off-road biking. Consider an energetic, athletic dog like a German shorthaired pointer (page 65), Australian shepherd (page 46), dalmatian (page 30), or boxer (page 81).

MOSTLY Bs
Relaxed to the Max
You're a laidback lounger who likes to keep calm and collected. Modern life is already stressful and chaotic, so you'd like to spend your quality time with a canine that's perfectly content to curl up on the couch and who doesn't require a lot of maintenance. Check out some easygoing dogs like a French bulldog (page 45), pug (page 61), greyhound (page 50), or Yorkshire terrier (page 102).

MOSTLY Cs
All in the Family
You're a busy parent who welcomes the idea of a dog as another beloved family member. Teaching a kid to care for a pet is a great way to instill values like responsibility and cooperation. Children can be a little rough with fragile small dogs, so go for someone sturdy and sweet-tempered. Labrador or golden retrievers (page 22 and page 70), French or English bulldogs (page 45 and page 37), huskies (page 62), and Saint Bernards (page 101) are all family-friendly furballs.

MOSTLY Ds
Extra, Extra!
You're urban, stylish, interesting, and perhaps a bit . . . high maintenance. You're not afraid to take on the challenges of a big-personality pooch if it means having a showstopping sidekick. Do you want to make a entrance with your adorable attention-grabbing bestie? A Cavalier King Charles spaniel (page 66), Pomeranian (page 38), Chihuahua (page 74), or shih tzu (page 85) is as adaptable and unique as you are!

Quick Rufference Guide

Size

EXTRA-SMALL
Brussels Griffon (page 21)
Chihuahua (page 74)
Pomeranian (page 38)
Shih Tzu (page 85)
Yorkshire Terrier (page 102)

SMALL
Beagle (page 73)
Boston Terrier (page 29)
Cavalier King Charles
    Spaniel (page 66)
Cocker Spaniel (page 57)
Corgi (page 82)
Dachshund (page 93)
French Bulldog (page 45)
Miniature Schnauzer
    (page 98)
Pug (page 61)
Shiba Inu (page 69)

MEDIUM
Airedale Terrier (page 77)
American Pit Bull Terrier
    (page 34)
Australian Shepherd
    (page 46)
Basset Hound (page 26)
Bull Terrier (page 90)
Chow Chow (page 58)
Dalmatian (page 30)

English Bulldog (page 37)
German Shorthaired
    Pointer (page 65)
Labradoodle (page 53)
Samoyed (page 49)
Shar-Pei (page 41)
Siberian Husky (page 62)
Standard Poodle (page 89)

LARGE
Bernese Mountain Dog
    (page 42)
Boxer (page 81)
Doberman Pinscher
    (page 97)
German Shepherd
    (page 54)
Golden Retriever (page 70)
Greyhound (page 50)
Irish Setter (page 25)
Komondor (page 94)
Labrador Retriever
    (page 22)
Old English Sheepdog
    (page 86)
Rottweiler (page 33)

EXTRA-LARGE
Great Dane (page 78)
Saint Bernard (page 101)

Shedding

LOTS OF SHEDDING
Australian Shepherd
(page 46)
Bernese Mountain Dog
(page 42)
Chow Chow (page 58)
Cocker Spaniel (page 57)
Corgi (page 82)
German Shepherd
(page 54)
Golden Retriever (page 70)
Labrador Retriever
(page 22)
Old English Sheepdog
(page 86)
Rottweiler (page 33)
Saint Bernard (page 101)
Samoyed (page 49)
Siberian Husky (page 62)

SOME SHEDDING
Basset Hound (page 26)
Bull Terrier (page 90)
Cavalier King Charles
Spaniel (page 66)
Dalmatian (page 30)
German Shorthaired
Pointer (page 65)
Great Dane (page 78)

Irish Setter (page 25)
Pomeranian (page 38)
Pug (page 61)
Shiba Inu (page 69)

LOW SHEDDING
Airedale Terrier (page 77)
American Pit Bull Terrier
(page 34)
Beagle (page 73)
Boston Terrier (page 29)
Boxer (page 81)
Brussels Griffon (page 21)
Chihuahua (page 74)
Dachshund (page 93)
Doberman Pinscher
(page 97)
English Bulldog (page 37)
French Bulldog (page 45)
Greyhound (page 50)
Komondor (page 94)
Labradoodle (page 53)
Miniature Schnauzer
(page 98)
Shar-Pei (page 41)
Shih Tzu (page 85)
Standard Poodle (page 89)
Yorkshire Terrier (page 102)

Energy Levels

HIGH ENERGY
American Pit Bull Terrier
(page 34)
Australian Shepherd
(page 46)

Beagle (page 73)
Boxer (page 81)
Bull Terrier (page 90)
Corgi (page 82)
Dalmatian (page 30)

Family Friendly

Long Life Expectancy

Australian Shepherd
(page 46)
Beagle (page 73)
Brussels Griffon (page 21)
Cavalier King Charles
Spaniel (page 66)
Chihuahua (page 74)
Dachshund (page 93)
Irish Setter (page 25)
Labradoodle (page 53)

Labrador Retriever
(page 22)
Miniature Schnauzer
(page 98)
Pomeranian (page 38)
Pug (page 61)
Shiba Inu (page 69)
Shih Tzu (page 85)
Standard Poodle (page 89)
Yorkshire Terrier (page 102)

Barking Tendencies

ALWAYS BARKING

Basset Hound (page 26)
Beagle (page 73)
Brussels Griffon (page 21)
Chihuahua (page 74)
Corgi (page 82)
Dachshund (page 93)
Miniature Schnauzer
(page 98)
Pomeranian (page 38)
Samoyed (page 49)
Siberian Husky (page 62)
Standard Poodle (page 89)
Yorkshire Terrier (page 102)

BARK ONLY TO ALERT

Boston Terrier (page 29)
Chow Chow (page 58)
English Bulldog (page 37)
French Bulldog (page 45)
Golden Retriever (page 70)
Pug (page 61)
Rottweiler (page 33)
Saint Bernard (page 101)

ABOUT THE AUTHOR

Melissa Maxwell has edited and authored many different books. She lives in Brooklyn, New York.

ABOUT THE ILLUSTRATOR

Sara Mulvanny has worked on a wide range of projects from books and magazines to large-scale illustrations for museums and restaurants. When not in her studio, she loves to go for walks in the surrounding countryside with Mabel, her Airedale puppy. You can check out her work at saramulvanny.com.